watch the falling

autumn leaves

Big trees, little trees
climbing high,
leaves stretched up
toward the sky.

Trees lived on
Earth long before
the dinosaurs did.

Apples, bananas, hazelnuts,
mangoes, coconuts, cherries...

Contents

The biggest trees in
the world are the giant
sequoias in the US.
One tree is so big that
an arch has been cut
through the trunk and
cars drive through it!

...all these foods
come from trees.

seed

I know what

There are three main
types of tree in the world:

I know that trees
have leaves and
branches, but
what else is
there to know?

leaves

bark

roots

You often find
palm trees by
beaches in hot
countries.

Palm trees

These trees are found in hot
places. They have big, thick
leaves that protect them
from hot winds.

Trees are the biggest plants in the world.
Most of them grow much taller than us.

a tree is!

palm trees, coniferous trees, and deciduous trees.

Trees live much longer than we do. The oldest tree is over 4,000 years old and lives in California.

Coniferous trees

These trees have long, thin leaves called needles and have cones instead of flowers. They keep their leaves all year round.

Conifer

Fir cone

Deciduous trees

These trees have large, flat leaves. They produce flowers in the spring and they lose their leaves in the winter.

All trees have a trunk, leaves, branches, and long roots that stretch out underground.

5 years old

Now that it has grown, the oak tree makes its own **acorns.** Many acorns will be eaten by squirrels, but some will grow into trees.

The life of a tree

Have you ever seen acorns on an oak tree? These are its seeds. Every tree has seeds, which are **pocket-sized** plants, waiting to grow into more trees.

The seed

Trees grow from seeds. The seeds of an oak tree are called acorns.

3 days old

A seed will start to grow if it has air, water, and warmth.

3 weeks old

The new leaves soak up sunlight, which the tree turns into food.

Young

3 days old

Old

300 years old

7

Trees have roots that grow down underground, where it is damp and dark. Roots help to keep the tree upright and they also drink water from the soil, which trees need to live.

60 years old

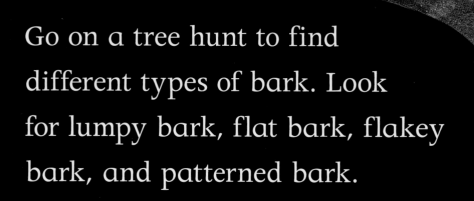

Go on a tree hunt to find different types of bark. Look for lumpy bark, flat bark, flakey bark, and patterned bark.

Rub, rub, rub

Take the crayon, lay it on its side, and rub it over the surface. The bark pattern will start to show through.

Compare them

Take bark rubbings from different trees and compare them. Use different colored crayons for different trees.

The best way to compare bark is to make lots of bark rubbings.

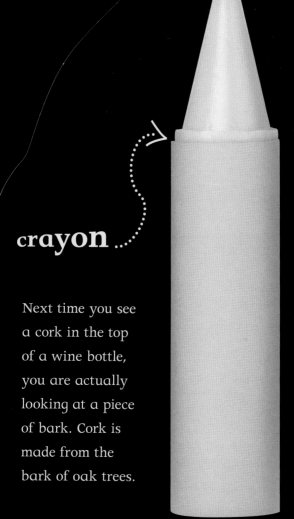

crayon

Next time you see a cork in the top of a wine bottle, you are actually looking at a piece of bark. Cork is made from the bark of oak trees.

Choose a tree

Find a big tree, lay a piece of plain white or construction paper on the bark, and tape it in place. Choose a colored crayon.

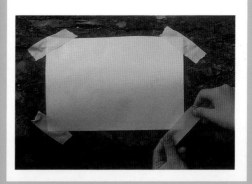

Let's go inside

Trees are covered in bark, which protects the **woody** trunk inside —a little like our skin protects us. Different trees have different bark; some is smooth, some is rough.

A tree for all seasons

Some trees have leaves that change color in the **fall** and then drop off. These are the deciduous trees that sleep in winter.

Leaves spread out over the summer months and use sunlight to make food for the tree.

In the spring, trees grow buds that will turn into leaves.

the bud

new leaves

10

Frosty snowflakes
settle on the branches.

Winter

The tree uses the food
that the leaves have
made over the summer to
live on through the cold
winter. It stands bare,
waiting for the warm
spring months.

Spring

In the spring the sun comes out and the new, strong leaves burst from their buds. The tree also produces flowers, often called blossom, which produce seeds for new trees.

Food factories

The leaves on the tree are the food factory. They stretch toward the sun and use the sunlight to help make food, which they pass down to the rest of the tree in the sap.

Believe it or not, the maple syrup that you put on your pancakes is sap from the sugar maple tree!

9

Chilly

decorations

Many Christmas tree decorations—wooden and cardboard ones—are also made from trees.

leaves

Conifers have needle-shaped leaves that are thin and hard so that they don't get damaged by the snow.

Christmas trees are grown on tree farms.

Pine trees are triangle-shaped to make sure that as many leaves as possible see the low-set sun to take in food.

Big trees give lots of shade.

Summer

In the summer the days are long and the tree is full of leaves working to make food. The flowers turn into seeds, ready to fall and make new trees.

The weather gets colder in the fall and the leaves turn amazing reds, browns, and oranges. The leaves die and begin to fall to the ground.

Fall

As the summer ends, the days get shorter and shorter. This is how the trees know to begin getting ready for **winter**.

old
leaves

In the fall there is less sun and the leaves stop making food. They dry out, which changes their color.

In the winter there are no leaves making food, but the tree is still alive and preparing to make new buds for the spring.

no
leaves

11

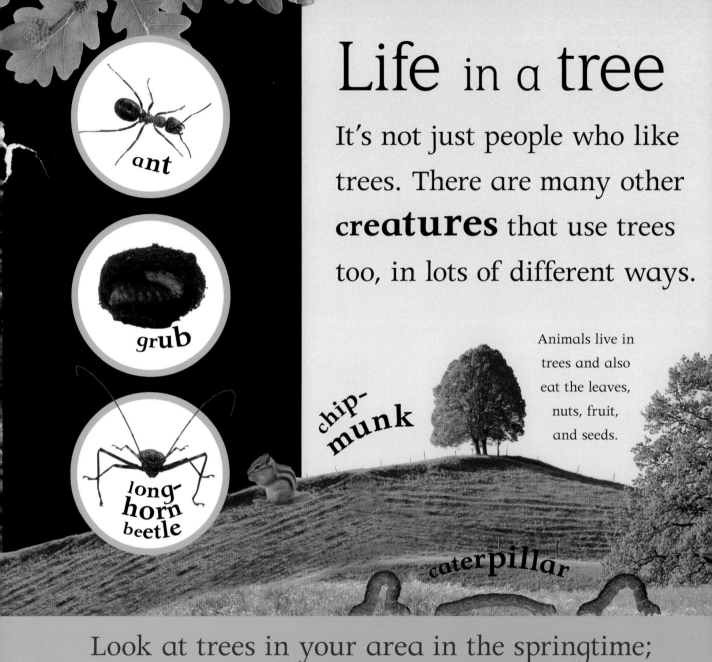

Life in a tree

It's not just people who like trees. There are many other **creatures** that use trees too, in lots of different ways.

ant

grub

long-horn beetle

chip-munk

caterpillar

Animals live in trees and also eat the leaves, nuts, fruit, and seeds.

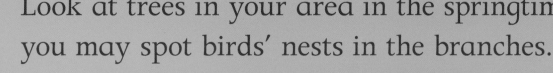

14 Look at trees in your area in the springtime; you may spot birds' nests in the branches.

trees

If you travel to the cold places of the world you will often find conifer forests. These trees are evergreen.

cone

seeds

Conifers don't have flowers, instead they have cones that hold seeds. When a cone falls it is often open and the seeds have dropped out.

Conifers like hot and cold weather

Conifers live in hot places too, but are particularly good in chilly places.

Evergreen means that the trees keep their leaves all year round. They don't lose them in the winter.

Conifer leaves are called needles.

A city
of trees

en the flap to find the
den rain forest animals.

wood

It is important that we grow new trees when we cut them down, or we will run out.

The wood is sent all over the world and turned into things like houses or toys.

From forest to home

In orde[r]
us to use
we have
them d[o]

Huge areas of rain forest are cut down each year to provide wood for people.

chainsaw

owl

When a tree dies and falls down, many plants and animals still use the logs as their homes.

Many animals munch away on the leaves of trees. Some trees make a second set of leaves in the summer to replace eaten ones.

acorn weevil

The acorn weevil makes a hole in an acorn and lays its eggs inside. When the babies are born they eat the nut inside.

One old oak tree could hold 300 types of insect living and feeding on it.

15

A life without trees

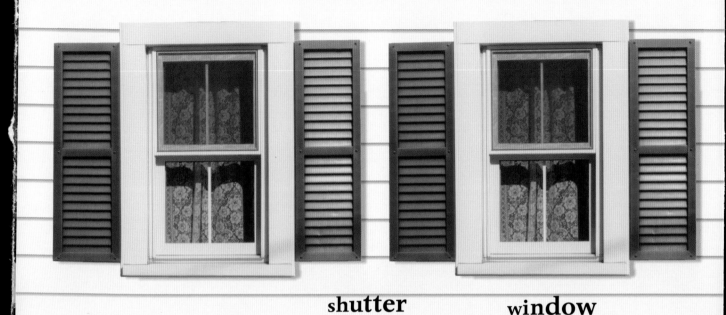

shutter   **window**

Look around your home and try to imagine a life without trees. It wouldn't be just your **backyard** that would look different.

Tables, chairs, building blocks, cupboards, toybox, favorite books—are they all trees?

snake

Many snakes live in trees, so watch out!

butterfly

jaguar

The jaguar snoozes on branches. Its coat helps it hide in the trees so that no animals can see it.

These liza[r] live in trees ab[o] water.

ig

bat

frog

orangutan

...ds
...ve

...uana

These apes make
nests in the trees to sleep in.
They leap from
tree to tree to
find food.

Trees grow best in rainy places. Some places have so much **rain** that you can hardly see for the trees. These areas are called rain forests.

The rain-forest trees are used by hundreds of animals. Jungles are giant animal cities.

17

LONDON, NEW YORK, MUNICH,
MELBOURNE, and DELHI

Written and edited by
Penelope Arlon
Designed by
Tory Gordon-Harris

DTP Designer Almudena Díaz
Production Claire Pearson
Publishing managers
Sue Leonard and Jo Connor

Published in the United States by DK Publishing, Inc.
375 Hudson Street, New York, NY 10014

06 07 08 09 10   10 9 8 7 6 5 4 3 2 1

A Cataloging-in-Publication record for this book is
available from the Library of Congress.

ISBN-10: 0-7566-1773-1
ISBN-13: 978-0-7566-1773-8

Color reproduction by Media Development
and Printing, United Kingdom
Printed and bound in China by
Hung Hing Printing Co., Ltd

Discover more at
www.dk.com

INDEX

Bonsai tree

Trees all around

staircase

A lot of your house is made of wood too. Floorboards, stairs, and many ceiling beams are wooden.

toilet paper

toys

If there were no trees, you wouldn't even have any toilet paper! It's made from pulped-up wood.

It's not just your pencil that is made of wood. Erasers also come from trees—they are made from sap.

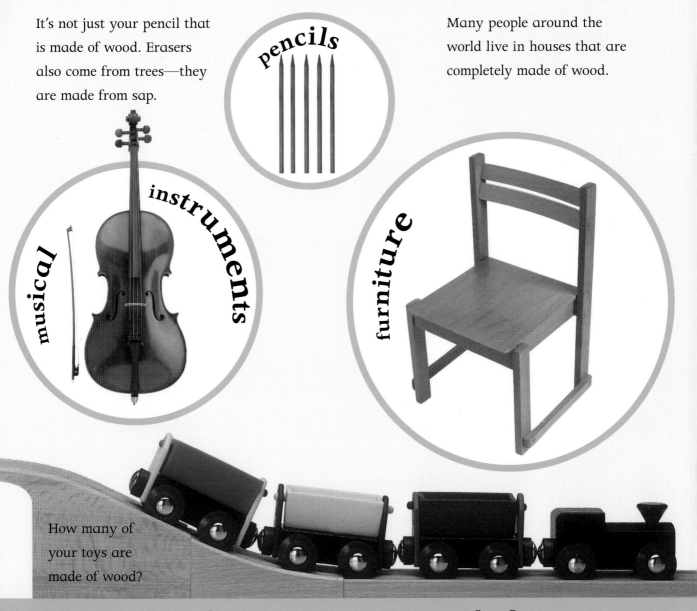

pencils

Many people around the world live in houses that are completely made of wood.

musical instruments

furniture

How many of your toys are made of wood?

Some musical instruments are made from wood—such as violins, clarinets, and pianos.

Wood comes from trees. So if there were no trees you wouldn't have any **wooden** furniture, or doors, or even books—they are made from wood too.

house

decoration

door

What would your backyard or local park look like without trees?